Train Your Brain with Problem-Solving Activities

THINK LIKE A PROGRAMMER

by Emilee Hillman

illustrated by Dana Regan

Published in 2020 by Cavendish Square Publishing, LLC
243 5th Avenue, Suite 136, New York, NY 10016

Copyright © 2020 by Cavendish Square Publishing, LLC

First Edition

No part of this publication may be reproduced, stored in a retrieval system, or transmitted in any form or by any means—electronic, mechanical, photocopying, recording, or otherwise—without the prior permission of the copyright owner. Request for permission should be addressed to Permissions, Cavendish Square Publishing, 243 5th Avenue, Suite 136, New York, NY 10016. Tel (877) 980-4450; fax (877) 980-4454.

Website: cavendishsq.com

This publication represents the opinions and views of the author based on his or her personal experience, knowledge, and research. The information in this book serves as a general guide only. The author and publisher have used their best efforts in preparing this book and disclaim liability rising directly or indirectly from the use and application of this book.

All websites were available and accurate when this book was sent to press.

Library of Congress Cataloging-in-Publication Data

Names: Hillman, Emilie, author. | Regan, Dana, illustrator.
Title: Train your brain with problem-solving activities / Emilee Hillman ; illustrator, Dana Regan.
Description: First edition. | New York : Cavendish Square, 2020. | Series: Think like a programmer | Audience: Grades 2-5. | Includes bibliographical references and index.
Identifiers: LCCN 2018054572 (print) | LCCN 2018060920 (ebook) | ISBN 9781502648051 (ebook) | ISBN 9781502648044 (library bound) | ISBN 9781502648020 (pbk.) | ISBN 9781502648037 (6 pack)
Subjects: LCSH: Computer programming--Juvenile fiction. | Computer science--Juvenile literature. | Problem solving--Juvenile literature.
Classification: LCC QA76.52 (ebook) | LCC QA76.52 .H55 2020 (print) | DDC 005.1--dc23
LC record available at https://lccn.loc.gov/2018054572

Editorial Director: David McNamara
Editor: Kristen Susienka
Copy Editor: Nathan Heidelberger
Associate Art Director: Alan Sliwinski
Designer: Joe Parenteau
Illustrator: Dana Regan
Production Coordinator: Karol Szymczuk

Printed in the United States of America

Contents

INTRODUCTION 4
ACTIVITY ATTRIBUTES 6
EVENT COORDINATORS 8
MODEL HOME 10
TURTLE TANK 12
WRITING THE RULES 14
A DETAILED BREAKFAST 16
PIZZA SOLUTIONS 18
FIXING UP THE CLASS 20
PROBLEM-SOLVING PRO 22
THE ORDER OF A DAY 24
STEPS TO A SNOWMAN 26
SHAPE UNKNOWN 28
GLOSSARY 30
FIND OUT MORE 31
INDEX 32

Introduction

You want to be a computer programmer—great! These activities will help you sharpen your problem-solving skills. The best programmers know you have to understand a problem before you can solve it. This means you have to figure out what the problem is. Programmers do this by breaking a big problem into smaller problems. Once you understand each part, you can solve the bigger problem.

This is all part of **computational thinking**. Despite the name, this way of thinking doesn't need a computer! All you have to do is think about how to solve problems, one step at a time.

These fun activities will help you train your brain to identify and break down problems. You'll also learn that some solutions are better than others. That is why it's important to understand and practice this thinking. This is how you learn to think like a programmer!

Activity Attributes

NUMBER OF PLAYERS 2

TIME NEEDED

15–20 minutes

You'll Need
- Pencil
- Paper

ACTIVITY OVERVIEW

Describing a problem is an important part of computer science. This is called **problem definition**. Programmers must first describe a problem before they can find a solution! **Debuggers** do this too. This involves thinking hard about something familiar. In this activity, you and a friend will think about your favorite hobbies. You will figure out what you need to be good at them!

INSTRUCTIONS

Get together with a partner. Each of you should think of an activity that you like to do. This could be a sport, playing a video game, or something

else. Use a piece of paper and a pencil to write down your answers. Pick one answer to talk about. Once you and your partner have an activity in mind, make another list. This time, the list should be about things you think someone needs to do the activity well. After you both have completed your list of things, compare answers. Repeat this with other ideas.

THINK ABOUT IT!

It's not always easy to think of ideas. Sometimes we need help. This activity helps you work with others and think of ideas together. In computer programming, a problem can have many correct answers. Usually, many programmers have to work together to find the best solution. This is why it is good to learn how to work with others on problems.

Event Coordinators

NUMBER OF PLAYERS 2

TIME NEEDED
20–30 minutes

> **You'll Need**
> - Pencil
> - Paper

ACTIVITY OVERVIEW

Programmers use a lot of computational thinking. That means they break down a big problem into smaller tasks. Each small task they finish helps get to the next small task. Once every small task is completed, the big problem is solved. You can practice computational thinking right now. In this activity, you and a friend will plan an event.

INSTRUCTIONS

With a friend, pretend you are planning an event for school. Write down what event you are planning. Together, write down some problems you might face when planning the event. Will there be food? How will you get the food to the event? If

there is music, what kind of music will you play? Will you send invitations, or can anyone join the event? Once you have a list, divide the problems equally between you two. Come up with solutions to the problems. Write your ideas down separately. Once you have answers for every problem on your list, share them with your friend.

Model Home

NUMBER OF PLAYERS

TIME NEEDED

20–30 minutes

ACTIVITY OVERVIEW

Problem solving has many steps. The first step is called **problem decomposition**. This is when you break down your big problem into small tasks. Problem decomposition is a major part of computational thinking, but it is only the first step of the larger problem-solving process. After breaking down a problem, it is important to come up with solutions, try them out, and write down the results. That way, you can find the best way to fix the problem. In this activity, you will build a strong house.

You'll Need
- Pencil
- Drawing supplies
- Paper
- Tape
- Building materials (such as Styrofoam, cardboard, construction paper, etc.)

INSTRUCTIONS

You might know the story of the Three Little Pigs. In it, three pigs build houses. Each house is made of different materials. The pigs are trying to build houses that can stand up even after a big scary wolf tries to blow them down. Only the strongest house stays standing.

In this activity, you will build your own house, just like the little pigs. First, write at the top of a piece of paper what you are trying to do. Then, draw what your house will look like. What will it be made of? Make a list of materials you will use to build your house. Then, build your house. Once you are done, ask an adult or a friend to pretend they are the wolf trying to blow the house down. What happens to the house? Is it strong enough to stay standing? Write down why your design worked or didn't work.

Turtle Tank

NUMBER OF PLAYERS

TIME NEEDED

30–45 minutes

You'll Need
- Pencil
- Drawing supplies
- Paper

ACTIVITY OVERVIEW

Figuring out how to break down a problem is a big part of computational thinking, but it isn't always easy to do. Sometimes, you need to do more research to find a solution to a problem. In this activity, you will pretend to take care of a turtle.

INSTRUCTIONS

Imagine that your class is getting a pet turtle. Your teacher asks you to set up the turtle's tank. How do you do this? First, you have to find out what turtles like in their tanks. Go online to research turtle tanks. Write down any ideas that might be good to add to your turtle's tank. What are some important things turtles need to live comfortably? Once you have your list, draw what your turtle tank will look like. Write a few sentences about each part of the tank. How does everything help the turtle live comfortably?

Writing the Rules

NUMBER OF PLAYERS 1

TIME NEEDED

15–20 minutes

You'll Need
- Pencil
- Paper

ACTIVITY OVERVIEW

Coders often have to design programs or computer languages by breaking a big problem down into smaller parts. They do this so that they can understand what they have to do before they do it. Just like in sports, they want to know the rules before they start. In this activity, you will write the rules to one of your favorite games.

INSTRUCTIONS

Imagine your favorite game to play outside. Is it hide and seek? Ghosts in the graveyard? Red rover? Now, think of how you play the game. Write down the game's rules. Pretend you have to write the rules for someone who has never played the game before. What rules will you tell them? Are there any special instructions? When you write down the rules, be as detailed as possible. If the game needs certain materials to play it, add those in too. Make sure each step is written in order. Afterward, read what you've written. Could you follow your instructions to play the game?

A Detailed Breakfast

NUMBER OF PLAYERS

TIME NEEDED
15–20 minutes

You'll Need
- Pencil
- Paper

ACTIVITY OVERVIEW

All computer programs need instructions to work. Instructions break down one big task into smaller tasks. You can do this with your tasks at home too. Simpler steps make big problems easier to solve. In this activity, you will break down a breakfast meal into smaller steps.

INSTRUCTIONS

Imagine a friend comes over to your house one morning. They tell you they have never eaten cereal before! They ask you how you make a bowl of cereal. Get a piece of paper and think of what your answer would be. Write out the steps. Be as

detailed as possible. Make sure your steps are in the right order, or else your friend might be confused. When you're done with these instructions, think of other instructions. How would you make your favorite meal? Write those instructions down too!

Pizza Solutions

NUMBER OF PLAYERS 1

TIME NEEDED

15–20 minutes

You'll Need
- Pencil
- Paper

ACTIVITY OVERVIEW

Many people working in coding take a big task and break it into smaller tasks. Smaller tasks are easier to finish. They also help lead to solving the bigger task. In this activity, you will plan a pizza party.

INSTRUCTIONS

Imagine you want to have a pizza party. What do you need for it to be a success? Do you need pizza? What about family members or friends to come to the party? What is your pizza made of? How will you serve the pizza? Write down your ideas on a piece of paper. When that's done, maybe ask your mom, dad, or an adult if you can really throw your pizza party!

Fixing Up the Class

NUMBER OF PLAYERS 1

TIME NEEDED

15–20 minutes

> **You'll Need**
> - Pencil
> - Drawing supplies
> - Paper

ACTIVITY OVERVIEW

Programmers are often asked to find simple solutions to tough problems. However, they sometimes have to find a solution to a problem they don't even know! Identifying a problem to be solved is a key part of computational thinking. In this activity, you will create a solution to an **organizational** problem. An organizational problem is one that needs your help to put materials in order.

INSTRUCTIONS

First, think of an organizational problem you might have at school. Some examples are lost homework, messy markers, or books falling off shelves. Next,

think of ways you might solve this problem. Write your ideas down. Finally, draw a picture of your solutions and share them with your class, some friends, or an adult.

Problem-Solving Pro

NUMBER OF PLAYERS

TIME NEEDED

15–20 minutes

You'll Need
- Pencil
- Paper

ACTIVITY OVERVIEW

Computer programs follow directions. These directions are called **procedures**. Every day, you follow directions too. Following directions is an important part of computer coding. By following directions in order, computers and coders can find and fix any problem. To solve a problem, people use these steps:

1. Define the problem.
2. Think of solutions.
3. Pick a solution.
4. Test the solution.
5. Review results.

In this activity, you will break down a problem and solve it by following directions.

INSTRUCTIONS

First, think of a problem you can solve. It can be something like finishing your homework, making a sandwich, inventing a new game, or pouring a glass of water. After you have a problem in mind, think about how you can solve it. What things do you need? Follow the five steps listed under Activity Overview. You can imagine the last two steps if you need to. Make sure you follow the steps in order. That will help you solve the problem correctly.

The Order of a Day

NUMBER OF PLAYERS 2 OR MORE

TIME NEEDED

20–30 minutes

ACTIVITY OVERVIEW

You'll Need
- Pencil
- Paper
- Scissors

It's important to follow directions. Computer programs have to follow directions too. These directions are called procedures. Each procedure must be done in the right order. If followed correctly, the procedures will help you complete your task. In this activity, you and your partner will think about what your tasks mean and how to put them in order.

INSTRUCTIONS

You and your partner should think of different activities you do in a day. This can be tasks like brushing your teeth, waking up, eating breakfast, or going to school. Write these ideas down on a piece of paper. Make sure each activity is written with space around it to cut out later. After you have your list, cut each activity into a square flash card. Once you have all the cards, make a small pile with them. Turn the cards over so you and your partner don't see the words. Then, take turns choosing a card and acting out the activity. You can't use any words, though, only gestures! Whoever isn't acting should guess the activity. After you have guessed all the cards, flip them over so you can see what they are and put them in order. What is the first activity you do in a day? What is the last?

Steps to a Snowman

NUMBER OF PLAYERS 1

TIME NEEDED

15–20 minutes

You'll Need
- Pencil
- Drawing supplies
- Paper

ACTIVITY OVERVIEW

Every day, you carry out tasks. Some tasks are easy. Other tasks are hard. Each task has different steps to follow. Do you ever think about the steps of walking or eating food? What about building things? In this activity, you will think about building a snowman.

INSTRUCTIONS

First, imagine your snowman. What is he like? Next, write out the steps for building your snowman. What materials will you need? When you are done writing your answers, draw one picture that shows each step of building the snowman. Afterward,

look at your drawings. Are they in order and easy to understand? If you don't want to draw each step, you could also use Play-Doh or LEGOs to imagine each step of building your snowman.

Shape Unknown

NUMBER OF PLAYERS

TIME NEEDED

20–30 minutes

> **You'll Need**
> - Pencil
> - Drawing supplies
> - Paper

ACTIVITY OVERVIEW

Sometimes, explaining the steps of a problem can be tough. This is true when trying to solve a new problem. Coders usually break problems into smaller tasks. These smaller tasks are simpler to follow. Each step completed gets them closer to solving the final answer. In this activity, you and a friend will try to figure out each other's visions.

INSTRUCTIONS

You and a friend should think of different shapes. Some examples are triangles, octagons, trees, flowers, or the sun. Write your list down. Then, you and your friend should each choose one shape from the list. Don't tell each other what shape you chose, though. After you have a shape in mind, write out instructions for how to draw your shape. Then swap instructions with your friend. Can you follow the instructions to draw their shape? What shape did you have to draw? Did your friend draw your shape? If not, how could you have made your instructions clearer?

Glossary

CODER A person who works on computer programs; also called a programmer.

COMPUTATIONAL THINKING A way of thinking where you break a big task into smaller tasks.

DEBUGGER A person who works on fixing problems in computer programs.

ORGANIZATIONAL A word that describes putting things in a certain order.

PROBLEM DECOMPOSITION Breaking down a big problem into smaller, simpler ones.

PROBLEM DEFINITION Describing a problem.

PROCEDURE A series of steps for solving a problem or completing a task.

Find Out More

BOOKS

Briggs, Jason R. *Python for Kids: A Playful Introduction to Programming*. San Francisco, CA: No Starch Press, 2013.

Woodcock, Jon. *Coding Games in Scratch: A Step-by-Step Visual Guide to Building Your Own Computer Games*. New York: DK Children, 2015.

WEBSITE

Tynker: Coding for Kids

http://www.tynker.com

This website gives children access to key apps and games that help them learn about coding.

VIDEO

Coding for Kids: What Is Computer Coding?

https://www.youtube.com/watch?v=THOEQ5soVpY

This video explains what computer programming is and what depends on computer programs to work.

Index

Entries in **boldface** are glossary terms.

coder, 14, 22, 28
computational thinking, 5, 8, 10, 12, 20
debugger, 6
group activities, 6–7, 8–9, 24–25, 28–29
individual activities, 10–11, 12–13, 14–15, 16–17, 18–19, 20–21, 22–23, 26–27
order, 15, 17, 20, 22–23, 24–25, 27
organizational, 20
planning, 8–9, 11, 18–19, 26–27

problem decomposition, 4–5, 8–9, 10–11, 12–13, 14–15, 16–17, 18–19, 23, 24–25, 26–27, 28–29
problem definition, 4–5, 6–7, 8–9, 11, 14–15, 20–21, 22–23
procedure, 16–17, 22–23, 25–26, 27–27, 28–29
programmer, 4–5, 6–7, 8, 14, 20, 22, 28
research, 12–13
rules, 14–15
steps, 5, 10, 16–17, 22–23, 26–27, 28–29
testing solutions, 5, 7, 10–11, 22–23, 29
working together, 7